More Drama Workshops for Young Children

10 Drama Workshops for Young Children based on Children's Stories

by

Julie Meighan

First published in 2024

By

JemBooks

Cork,

Ireland

dramastartbooks.com

All rights reserved.

No part of this book may be reproduced or utilised in any form or by any electronic, digital or mechanical means, including information storage, photocopying, filming, recording, video recording and retrieval systems, without prior permission in writing from the publisher. The only exception is by a reviewer, who may quote short excerpts in a review. The moral rights of the author have been asserted.

ISBN: 978-1-0687433-0-6

About the Author

Julie Meighan is a lecturer in Drama in Education at the Cork Institute of Technology. She has taught Drama to all age groups and levels. She is the author of the Amazon bestselling *Drama Start: Drama Activities, Plays and Monologues for Young Children (Ages 3 -8)* ISBN 978-0956896605, *Drama Start Two: Drama Activities and Plays for Children (Ages 9-12)* ISBN 978-0-9568966-1-2 and *Stage Start: 20 Plays for Children (Ages 3-12)* ISBN 978-0956896629.

Contents

About the Author 3

Drama Techniques Glossary 5

The Ugly Duckling Drama Workshop 12

The Magic Porridge Pot Drama Workshop 17

Jack and the Beanstalk Drama Workshop 23

The Elves and the Shoemaker Drama Workshop 29

The Town Mouse and the Country Mouse Drama Workshop 38

The Frog Prince Drama Workshop 41

Little Red Riding Hood Drama Workshop 45

The North Wind and the Sun Drama Workshop 52

The Little Red Hen Drama Workshop 56

The Crow and The Pitcher Drama Workshop 60

Drama Techniques Glossary

Action Narration:

- **What It Is:** Describing characters' actions and feelings out loud as they happen in a story.
- **Why Use It:** Helps children develop language skills, think creatively, and learn to express emotions. It encourages imagination and understanding by letting them visualize stories in action.
- **How to Use It:** While reading a story or creating one together, pause to describe what characters are doing and feeling. Encourage children to act out parts of the story as you narrate their actions and emotions.

Conscience Alley:

- **What It Is:** A pathway formed by two lines of children, offering contrasting advice to a character (another child or the teacher) who walks between them.
- **Why Use It:** Encourages children to consider different perspectives and make decisions, fostering empathy and critical thinking.
- **How to Use It:** Present a moral dilemma from a story. Have children stand in two lines and express different viewpoints or advice about the dilemma as a character walk through, contemplating their decision.

Flashback/Flashforward:

- **What It Is:** Temporarily stepping back into the past or jumping into the future within a story.

- **Why Use It:** Deepens understanding of story characters and plots, encourages creative thinking about consequences and possibilities.
- **How to Use It:** When telling a story, pause and guide children to imagine a character's past or future. Use props or simple visual aids to help them visualize and discuss the impact of these time shifts on the story.

Hot Seating:

- **What It Is:** One child pretends to be a character from a story, sitting in a "hot seat" to answer questions from their peers.
- **Why Use It:** Builds empathy, encourages deep thinking about characters' motivations and feelings, and enhances speaking and listening skills.
- **How to Use It:** After reading a story, select a character and a child to represent that character. Have other children ask questions. The child in the "hot seat" responds as if they are that character, using imagination to infer feelings and thoughts.

Improvisation:

- **What It Is:** Making up a scene or story on the spot without a script.
- **Why Use It:** Fosters creativity, spontaneity, and collaboration. It allows children to explore ideas and express themselves freely.
- **How to Use It:** Provide a simple scenario or setting and let children create their own dialogue and actions. Encourage them to build on each other's ideas, promoting teamwork and communication.

Mantle of the Expert:

- **What It Is:** Children take on roles as experts in a particular

field to solve problems or explore topics within a fictional scenario.
- **Why Use It:** Promotes deep engagement with subjects, encouraging children to take ownership of their learning and develop problem-solving skills.
- **How to Use It:** Create a scenario where children are experts in a field relevant to their interests. Guide them through solving a problem or exploring a topic, asking open-ended questions to encourage thinking and creativity.

Mime:

- **What It Is:** Expressing a story or concept through body movements and facial expressions, without speaking.
- **Why Use It:** Enhances physical coordination and non-verbal communication skills. Encourages observation and creativity.
- **How to Use It:** Introduce a theme or emotion and have children convey it through mime. Use music or props to inspire their movements and expressions.

Movement:

- **What It Is:** Using dance and expressive movement to tell a story or convey emotions.
- **Why Use It:** Promotes physical expression, creativity, and emotional awareness. Helps children communicate ideas beyond words.
- **How to Use It:** Play music and guide children to move in ways that express different emotions or tell parts of a story. Encourage them to use space and interact with each other through movement.

Role on the Wall:

- **What It Is:** Drawing a character's outline on large paper, then filling in traits, thoughts, and feelings inside the outline, and facts or actions on the outside.

- **Why Use It:** Helps children understand and differentiate between internal and external characteristics of characters, fostering empathy and deeper character analysis.
- **How to Use It:** After reading a story or discussing a character, create a large outline of the character together. Ask children to contribute ideas about what the character thinks and feels (inside) and what they do or how others see them (outside).

Role Play:

- **What It Is:** Pretending to be characters from stories or scenarios, acting out roles in improvised settings.
- **Why Use It:** Develops understanding of different perspectives, enhances communication skills, and promotes creativity through storytelling.
- **How to Use It:** Set up a scenario or use a story the children are familiar with. Assign roles and let them act out the story or scenario, encouraging them to express their character's viewpoint and interact with others.

Sculpting:

- **What It Is:** One child shapes another child into a pose that expresses an emotion, idea, or character trait without words.
- **Why Use It:** Encourages non-verbal communication and creativity, helps children understand and express complex emotions and ideas through body language.
- **How to Use It:** In pairs, one child thinks of an emotion or idea and then gently guides their partner into a pose that expresses it. The rest of the group can guess what's being portrayed.

Soundscape:

- **What It Is:** Making an imaginary place using only sounds. Children can use their voices, hands, or things around the classroom to make sounds like rain, animals, or cars.
- **Why Use It:** Helps children listen better and work together. It makes stories feel more real and fun by adding sounds to the background.
- **How to Use It:** Choose a story or place and talk about what sounds you might hear there. Then, have the children make those sounds together. For example, if you're imagining a forest, some children can make bird sounds, while others can rustle their hands to sound like the wind.

Still Image:

- **What It Is:** Creating a frozen picture or tableau with a group of children to represent a scene, concept, or moment in time.
- **Why Use It:** Enhances observation skills, encourages cooperation, and allows children to explore and communicate complex ideas visually.
- **How to Use It:** Choose a moment from a story or a theme. Have the children work together to create a pose that captures that moment or theme, discussing what each person will do and how they will arrange themselves.

Storytelling:

- **What It Is:** Narrating a story using words, gestures, and facial expressions to convey the narrative, characters, and emotions.
- **Why Use It:** Develops language skills, creativity, and imagination. Encourages children to think about narrative structure and character development.

- **How to Use It:** Encourage children to tell a story, either one they know or a new one they create. Guide them to use expressive gestures and facial expressions to bring the story to life.

Talking Objects:

- **What It Is:** Giving personalities and voices to inanimate objects and incorporating them into storytelling or role play.
- **Why Use It:** Stimulates imagination, encourages creative thinking and problem-solving, and adds depth to storytelling.
- **How to Use It:** Select objects and brainstorm with children, what personalities and voices they might have. Use these objects in stories or plays, allowing them to interact with characters.

Teacher in Role:

- **What It Is:** The teacher or facilitator assumes a character role within a story or scenario, interacting with the children as that character.
- **Why Use It:** Engages children deeply, blurring the lines between teaching and learning, and encourages empathy and imagination.
- **How to Use It:** Choose a character relevant to the lesson. Enter the classroom in character and interact with the children, guiding the lesson or activity from within the role.

Thought Tracking:

- **What It Is:** Pausing action in role play or drama to express a character's thoughts out loud.
- **Why Use It:** Helps children understand and express the internal motivations and emotions of characters, enhancing empathy and storytelling skills.

- **How to Use It:** During role play or after posing a still image, tap children on the shoulder as a signal for them to express their character's inner thoughts or feelings.

The Ugly Duckling Drama Workshop

Each child finds a space and sits down. Each child or a group of children are assigned a specific word and a corresponding action. The narrator/teacher reads the story aloud, and when the children hear their word, they must jump up and do their actions. The words are in bold to assist the teacher.

Word: Movement

Duckling: Flap your arms like small wings.
Swan: Gracefully stretch your arms up and out, like large wings.
Water: Wave-like motion with hands.
Quack: Place hands at your mouth and make a quacking gesture.
Laugh: Hold your belly and laugh heartily.
Cry: Wipe your eyes as if crying.
Fly: Extend arms to the side and mime flying.
Beautiful: Frame your face with your hands and smile.
Mother Duck: Waddle around the room.
Seasons (Spring, Summer, Autumn, Winter): For Spring, bloom like a flower; for Summer, sun above head with hands; for Autumn, sway like a tree and drop leaves (hands); for Winter, shiver and wrap arms around self.

Once upon a time, a mother duck's eggs hatched. One egg, larger than the others, took longer to hatch. When it finally did, out came a **duckling** that looked quite different from the rest. He was much larger and did not quite fit in. Despite his efforts, the **duckling** was often left out, laughed at, and even ignored by his siblings and other farm animals.

Feeling unwanted, the **duckling** decided to leave the farm. He travelled through the **seasons**, facing many challenges. In **Spring**, he admired the flowers but felt as if he didn't belong among them. During the hot **Summer**, he swam in cool **water** but was still lonely. In **Autumn**, he watched the leaves fall, feeling just as lost. The **Winter** was the hardest, with cold winds and snow; the **duckling** struggled to find shelter and food.

Finally, after a long and harsh **Winter**, **Spring** returned, and the **duckling**, now grown, saw a group of beautiful **swans** on a lake. Wishing to be with creatures as lovely as them, he approached, expecting them to laugh or attack. To his surprise, they welcomed him. Looking at his reflection in the **water**, he realized he was not a **duckling** at all—he had grown into a beautiful **swan**. Realizing his worth and finding his true family, the **swan** flapped his **beautiful** wings in joy, ready to start a new life, surrounded by love and acceptance.

Warm up: The children sit in a circle while one person, the "it," walks around tapping heads, saying "Duck" with each tap. Randomly, "it" chooses someone by tapping them and saying "Swan" instead of "Duck." The "Swan" then rises and chases "it" around the circle, aiming to tag them before they can sit down in the "Swan's" spot. If "it" is tagged, they go again. If not, the "Swan" becomes the new "it." The game is a fun, active way to engage children in a physical warm up.

Main Focus: *Emotional Mime* - choose a scene from the story where the ugly duckling is feeling a strong emotion, such as loneliness or fear. Ask the children to work in pairs and create a short mime performance that depicts the emotion in the scene. Encourage the children to use their bodies and facial expressions to convey the emotion without using words.

Suggestion of scenes:

The First Moments in the Pond - The scene where the duckling, freshly hatched, finds himself in the pond and realizes he looks different from his siblings. He tries to fit in, only to face rejection, embodying confusion, and sadness.

Encounter with the Farm Animals - This moment captures the duckling's attempt to find belonging among the farm animals, only to be scared away by their mocking. It's a poignant expression of fear and isolation.

The Harsh Winter - Alone during the cold, harsh winter, the duckling struggles to survive. This scene is a powerful depiction of despair and loneliness, as he faces the elements alone. ***Reflection in the Water*** - When the duckling sees his reflection in the water and realizes he has grown into a beautiful swan, it's a moment rich with surprise and self-realization. This transformation brings a mix of joy and the shock of discovery.

Being Welcomed by the Swans - Finally accepted by the swans, the former duckling experiences acceptance and joy for the first time. This moment of being welcomed as one of them marks a poignant end to his journey of self-discovery.

Hot Seating - choose one child to play the role of the ugly duckling and sit in a "hot seat" in front of the group. The other children can take turns asking the ugly duckling questions about how they felt during different parts of the story. Encourage the children to use their imagination and empathy to think about how the ugly duckling might have felt and how they might have reacted to different situations.

Examples of questions – the following are some suggestions of open-ended questions.

How did you feel when the other ducks didn't want to play with you?

What was it like to see your reflection in the water for the first time?

Were you scared when you were all alone during the winter?

What did you think when the beautiful swans approached you?

How did you keep hoping when things seemed so difficult?

What was the happiest moment in your journey?

Did you ever want to give up? What kept you going?

How did you feel when you realized you had turned into a beautiful swan?

What would you say to the other animals who were mean to you now that you're a swan?

What's the most important thing you learned during your adventures?

Still Image - explain to the children that they are experts in the story of The Ugly Duckling. Ask the children to work in small groups to create a still image that represents a key moment or theme in the story. Encourage the children to think about the emotions and relationships between the characters in the scene.

Improvisation - divide the children into small groups and assign each group a different scene from the story. Ask the children to create a short role play based on the scene, using movement and improvisation to bring the story to life. Here are some examples of scenes from the story of the Ugly Duckling:

Suggestions of scenes:

- The mother duck sitting on her eggs, waiting for them to hatch.
- The other ducks laughing and making fun of the ugly duckling when he hatches because he looks different.
- The ugly duckling running away and encountering other animals who also reject him for being different.
- The ugly duckling growing and changing as he matures, eventually realizing that he is actually a swan.
- The swan joining a group of other swans and finally feeling accepted and at home.

Action Narration - choose a scene from the story where the ugly duckling is facing a challenge or obstacle. Ask the children to work in pairs to create a short narration that describes the action in the scene. Encourage the children to use descriptive language and to think about the emotions and motivations of the characters in the scene.

Example - In a place with lots of animals, there was one little duck who felt very alone. He looked different and wanted to find friends who liked him just the way he was. So, he decided to go on a big adventure to find a place where he could be happy and have friends. He was a bit scared but also very brave. He said goodbye to the old place and started walking, hoping to find a new home where everyone would be kind to him.

Closure: Ask the children to sit in a circle. Explain to the children that they are going to play a game called "The Ugly Duckling Circle." Go around the circle and ask each child to share something that makes them unique or special. After each child shares, the rest of the group can clap or snap their fingers to show their support and appreciation for the child's uniqueness. Once everyone has had a turn, ask the children to take a deep breath and thank them for sharing their stories.

The Magic Porridge Pot Drama Workshop

Each child finds a space and sits down. Each child or a group of children are assigned a specific word and a corresponding action. The narrator/teacher reads the story aloud, and when the children hear their word, they must jump up and do their actions. The words are in bold to assist the teacher.

Word: Movement

Stir: Pretend to stir a big pot with a spoon.

Boil: Jump up and down like bubbling porridge.

Eat: Mime scooping porridge with a spoon and eating it.

Open: Mime opening something wide.

Close: Mime closing something tightly.

Stop: Freeze and put your hands up.

Grow: Slowly rise from a crouched position to standing, reaching your arms up high.

Overflow: Wave arms outward and gently sway side to side, like porridge spilling over.

Once upon a time, there was a little girl who lived with her mother. They were very poor and had nothing to eat. One day, the little girl met a kind old woman who gave her a magical **pot**. "This is a magic porridge **pot**," said the woman. "Whenever you're hungry, say 'Cook, little **pot**, cook,' and it will make porridge. To make it **stop**, say 'Stop, little **pot**, stop.'"

Excited, the girl brought the **pot** home. She said, "**Cook**, little **pot**, **cook**!" and began to **stir**. Soon, the **pot** began to **boil**, and delicious porridge appeared. The girl and her mother **ate** until they were full. Then, the girl said, "**Stop**, little **pot**, **stop**."

One day, when the girl was out, her mother felt hungry. She remembered the **pot** and said, "**Cook**, little **pot**, **cook**." She **ate** her fill but then forgot how to make the **pot stop**. The porridge began to **grow** and **overflow**, filling the house!

When the girl returned, she saw the porridge **overflowing**. Quickly, she shouted, "**Stop**, little **pot**, **stop**!" And at once, the **pot** stopped cooking. They had to **open** all the doors to let the porridge out!

From that day on, they were careful to use the magic **pot** wisely, always remembering to say "**Stop**, little **pot**, **stop**" when they had enough. They lived happily ever after, never going hungry again.

Warm up: Gather the children in a large circle and introduce "Magic Moves," a dynamic physical warm-up game. Start by demonstrating a simple magical gesture, such as waving a wand or stirring a giant pot, and pair it with a magical phrase like "abracadabra." Pass the gesture to the child next to you, encouraging them to perform the move and add their own magical twist. Each child takes turns, adding to the sequence with their unique magical action and phrase, inspired by "The Magic Porridge Pot." This activity not only gets the children moving but also sparks their creativity and prepares them for storytelling.

Main Focus: *Conscience Alley* - divide the children into two lines facing each other, creating a "conscience alley." Explain that one child will walk through the alley while the others on either side will be the good part of the conscience and the bad part of the conscience. They whisper positive and negative comments or feelings to the child, based on the dilemmas below. The children can also make up their own dilemmas. Once the child has walked through the alley, ask them to share their thoughts and feelings about the experience.

The Magic Seeds – The child who is walking down the conscience alley discovers seeds that can grow anything overnight. The good side suggests growing food for the hungry or beautiful plants to cheer people up. The bad side suggests growing rare treasures for personal gain or invasive species that could harm the environment.

The Time-Traveling Hat - The child who is walking down the conscience alley discovers a hat that allows time travel, the good side encourages visiting historical moments to learn and bring back knowledge. The bad side suggests altering past events for personal benefit, risking unintended consequences.

The Shape-Shifter's Cloak - The child who is walking down the conscience alley discovers a cloak that grants the power to shape-shift into any living creature. The good side highlights understanding and empathy by experiencing life as other beings, promoting conservation. The bad side whispers ideas about using the power for spying, escaping responsibilities, or trickery.

The Book of Secrets - The child who is walking down the conscience alley discovers a book that contains the world's secrets. The good side proposes using the knowledge to solve unsolved mysteries, cure diseases, and prevent disasters. The bad side tempts with exploiting secrets for personal gain, blackmail, or gaining unfair advantages.

The Invisible Backpack - The child who is walking down the conscience alley discovers an invisible backpack can carry anything without weight. The good side suggests its use for delivering aid unnoticed or helping people in need discreetly. The bad side imagines uses of the backpack such as theft, smuggling, or evading responsibility.

Emotional Mime - choose a scene from the story where the magic porridge pot is overflowing or the characters are feeling a strong emotion, such as surprise or joy. Ask the children to work in pairs and create a short mime performance that depicts the emotion in the scene. Encourage the children to use their bodies and facial expressions to convey the emotion without using words.

Hot Seating - choose one child to play the role of the main character (Old Woman, Girl, Magic Porridge Pot) in the story and sit in a "hot seat" in front of the group. The other children can take turns asking the main character questions about how they felt during different parts of the story. Encourage the children to use their imagination and empathy to think about how the main character might have felt and how they might have reacted to different situations.

Examples of questions – the following are some suggestions of open-ended questions.

Questions for the Old Woman: How did you feel when you first discovered the magic porridge pot and realized what it could do?

What was your biggest worry about giving the pot to the girl?

Can you describe a time when the magic pot helped you the most?

How did you decide to share the secret of the pot with the girl?

Looking back, would you have done anything differently with the magic porridge pot?

Questions for the Girl: What went through your mind the first time you saw the pot overflowing with porridge?

How did you feel when you couldn't remember the words to stop the porridge pot?

What was the reaction of the people around you when they saw all the porridge?

Can you talk about a moment when you wished the pot would stop making porridge?

If you had the chance to use the magic porridge pot again, what would you do differently?

Question for the Porridge Pot: What is it like to have the power to make endless porridge? How do you feel about it?

How did you react inside when you were asked to stop making porridge but couldn't because the right words weren't used?

If you could choose, would you like to make something other than porridge? What would it be and why?

What do you think is the most important thing the old woman and the girl should learn from having you?

Were there times when you wished to be an ordinary pot? Why or why not?

Still Image - explain to the children that they are experts in the story of The Magic Porridge Pot. Ask the children to work in small groups to create a still image that represents a key moment or theme in the story. Encourage the children to think about the emotions and relationships between the characters in the scene.

Role Play and Improvisation - divide the children into small groups and assign each group a different scene from the story. Ask the children to create a short role play based on the scene, using movement and improvisation to bring the story to life. Encourage the children to work together to create a cohesive and engaging performance.

Here are some examples of different scenes from the story of The Magic Porridge Pot:

- The old woman discovers the magic porridge pot in the woods.
- The old woman tests the magic porridge pot at home, and it starts to overflow.
- The old woman tells her daughter about the magic porridge pot and how it works.

- The daughter forgets the magic words to stop the porridge pot from overflowing.
- The porridge fills up the house and spills out into the streets, causing chaos.
- The villagers gather around the house to see what is happening and try to help.
- The daughter remembers the magic words and the porridge stops flowing.
- The daughter and the old woman share the porridge with the villagers, and everyone is happy.

Closure: At the end of their workshop, the children gather in a circle and pass around a small pot, referred to as the "Magic Wish" pot. Each child holds the pot, thinks of a special wish they have, perhaps for a friend, for themselves, or for everyone. They share it aloud with the group. After every child has shared their wish, they participate in a collective breath, pretending to send their wishes into the sky so they might come true.

Jack and the Beanstalk Drama Workshop

Each child finds a space and sits down. Each child or a group of children are assigned a specific word and a corresponding action. The narrator/teacher reads the story aloud, and when the children hear their word, they must jump up and do their actions. The words are in bold to assist the teacher.

Word: Movement:

Beans: Hold your hands close together, palms up, as if cradling something small and precious. **Beanstalk**: Start crouched low and slowly rise up on your toes, stretching your arms above your head, intertwining your fingers to mime the growing beanstalk.

Climb: Make alternating motions with your arms and legs as if pulling yourself up a ladder, showing the effort of climbing.

Giant: Stand on your toes, arms raised high and wide, stomping your feet to make heavy, thudding sounds, embodying the giant's immense size.

Gold: Rub your hands together and then let them fall open as if watching gold spill out, reflecting the glitter and wealth.

Chicken: Tuck your elbows into your sides, flap your arms like wings, and take small, quick steps around, miming a chicken's movements.

Harp: Pretend to play a large harp, fingers gracefully plucking at invisible strings, moving your hands up and down in front of you.

Chop: Hold one arm out straight, the other hand miming an axe chopping down on the extended arm's forearm, showing the action of chopping the beanstalk.

In a village, there lived a young boy named Jack and his mother. Their cottage was cozy, but times were tough, and they struggled to make ends meet. One morning, Jack's mother handed him their last possession of value, a cow, and asked him to take it to market. With a heavy heart, Jack led the cow down the winding path, hoping for a good trade.

Along the way, Jack encountered a mysterious old man who offered him magic **beans** in exchange for the cow. Delighted by the promise of magic, Jack agreed, and with the **beans** carefully tucked in his pocket, he rushed home. His mother, however, was furious at the seemingly foolish trade and tossed the **beans** out the window in despair.

Overnight, a giant **beanstalk** grew from the **beans**, reaching up into the sky. Jack awoke to the marvel and, with a mix of excitement and curiosity, began to **climb** the towering plant. Higher and higher he climbed, until he reached a land above the clouds, where a massive castle loomed.

Inside the castle, Jack discovered it was home to a fearsome **giant**. Quiet as a mouse, Jack sneaked around, finding treasures unimaginable. First, he laid eyes on bags of **gold** coins, sparkling and inviting. With his heart racing, he filled his pockets with the **gold**.

Next, Jack stumbled upon a magical **chicken** that laid **golden eggs**. He couldn't believe his luck as he gently scooped up the chicken under his arm. But Jack's adventure didn't end there. He also found a beautiful **harp** with golden strings that played the most enchanting music. Mesmerized, Jack decided to take the **harp** as well.

However, as Jack attempted to leave with his treasures, the **harp** cried out, waking the **giant**. Jack ran as fast as he could, the **giant**'s thunderous steps close behind him. With the **giant** in pursuit, Jack **climbed** down the **beanstalk** with all his might.

Upon reaching the ground, Jack yelled to his mother for an axe. With no time to spare, he began to **chop** at the **beanstalk**. Thud! Thud! Thud! With a few mighty **chops**, the **beanstalk** came crashing down, bringing the **giant** to his doom.

Breathless and relieved, Jack and his mother gazed at the treasures before them. They were safe, and their lives would be forever changed. The magic **beans** had brought them adventure, but more importantly, they brought them a new beginning. From that day on, Jack and his mother lived a comfortable life, always remembering the incredible journey above the clouds.

And so, the story of Jack and the **beanstalk** reminds us that bravery, quick thinking, and a bit of magic can lead to extraordinary places.

Warm-up: *Movement Exploration* - ask the children to spread out in the space. Explain to them that you are going to call out different types of movements (e.g. walking, running, hopping, skipping, jumping, crawling, etc.) and they should move around the space using those movements. Encourage them to be creative and use their imaginations to make the movements bigger, smaller, faster, slower, etc. After a few minutes, stop the activity and bring the children back to the centre of the space.

Soundscape Creation - Transition into creating soundscapes. Divide the children into small groups and assign each group a scene from the story (e.g., the beanstalk growing, Jack climbing, inside the giant's castle). Each group creates sounds that represent their scene using their voices, bodies, and available instruments.

Main Focus: *Mantle of the Expert* - Explain to the children that they are going to become a team of experts on "Jack and the Beanstalk". Ask them to imagine that they are part of a team of explorers who have just discovered the giant's castle at the top of the beanstalk. Ask the children to think about what they might see, hear, smell, and feel as they explore the castle. Ask them to work together to come up with a plan to defeat the giant and help Jack get his treasure back.

Encourage them to use their imaginations and think creatively about how they could solve the problem. After a few minutes, bring the children back to the centre of the space.

Thought Tracking – the children are gathered into a circle by the teacher. A specific scene from the story is chosen, and a child is selected to stand in the centre as a character from that scene, such as Jack, the Giant, or the Beanstalk itself. The teacher leads a discussion on the range of emotions the character might experience during the scene, like excitement, fear, happiness, or surprise. One by one, children approach the central figure, each gently tapping their shoulder and whispering an emotion. Upon receiving each whispered emotion, the central child expresses it using only body movements, without speaking. The surrounding circle of peers watches attentively, ready to guess the emotion being portrayed. After several turns of acting and guessing, another child steps into the centre to become a new character in a different scene, allowing the cycle of exploration and empathy to continue.

Character suggestions:

Jack

The Giant

The Magic Beanstalk

Jack's Mother

The Golden Goose

The Magic Harp

Suggested emotions:

Excited: The thrill of discovering the magic beans or the beanstalk reaching into the clouds.

Scared: The fear of meeting the Giant or hearing his thunderous voice.

Brave: The courage it takes for Jack to climb the beanstalk or to face the Giant.

Surprised: The astonishment of finding a castle in the sky or a goose that lays golden eggs.

Happy: The joy of Jack finding the golden treasures or reuniting with his mother.

Lonely: How Jack might feel being away from home or how the Giant feels in his castle in the sky.

Curious: The wonder of exploring a new, magical world above the clouds.

Relieved: The feeling when Jack safely returns home with the treasures.

Flashback/Flashforward - ask the children to think about a scene from "Jack and the Beanstalk" Ask them to imagine what might have happened before that scene (flashback) or what might happen after that scene (flashforward). Divide the children into groups and assign each group a different scene to work with. Ask them to create a short scene that shows the flashback or flashforward. Encourage them to be creative and use their imaginations to come up with interesting ideas. After a few minutes, ask each group to share their scene with the rest of the class. Here are some examples of scenes from Jack and the Beanstalk:

- Jack trading the cow for magic beans.
- Jack climbing up the beanstalk to reach the giant's castle.
- Jack meeting the giant's wife.
- Jack sneaking around the giant's castle.
- Jack stealing the golden goose and the magical harp.
- The giant chasing Jack down the beanstalk.
- The beanstalk being cut down and the giant falling to his death.

Closure: *Magic Beans Hunt* - explain to the children that the magic beans from the story of Jack and the Beanstalk have been scattered throughout the room and it's their job to find them. Allow the children to search for the beans, either individually or in small groups. Once all of the beans have been found, bring the group together and ask them to share what they remember about the story and the themes it explored, such as courage, greed, and consequences. Encourage the children to share how they can apply these themes to their own lives and challenges they may face. Conclude the workshop by reminding the children of the power of imagination and the importance of using their creativity to solve problems and make positive choices.

The Elves and the Shoemaker Drama Workshop

Gather all the children in a circle. Once everyone is seated and comfortable, introduce the story of "The Elves and the Shoemaker." The teacher explains that they will tell the story, and also describe movements that the children will act out together. Emphasize that their movements will help bring the story to life.

Movement Story:

Teacher: Once upon a time, in a small, cozy workshop filled with the scent of leather and wood shavings, there lived a shoemaker. He worked with all his might but was **struggling** to make ends meet (*everyone **pushes** and **pulls** as if working hard against an invisible force*). As night fell, he laid out his last piece of leather, hoping to craft a pair of shoes that could turn his fortunes (*everyone **smooths** out the floor in front of them, then **traces** the outline of a shoe with their fingers*).

Exhausted from his efforts, the shoemaker went to bed, leaving the unfinished leather on his workbench. Under the glow of the moonlight, tiny, mysterious elves **sneaked** into the shoemaker's workshop (*everyone **tiptoes** around quietly, fingers to lips*). These elves were **quick** and **nimble**, and they began to work **stitching**, **sewing**, and **hammering** away with incredible speed and skill (*everyone mimes **stitching** in the air, **sewing** with large, sweeping arm movements, and **hammering** with one hand striking the other palm*).

By morning, the shoemaker was met with a wonderful surprise—a beautifully made pair of shoes sat finished on his workbench. His astonishment turned to joy as he sold the shoes and was able to buy more materials (*everyone shows a **surprised** face, then **jumps for joy***). With the secret help of the elves, the shoemaker's fortunes improved. In gratitude, the shoemaker and his wife decided to craft tiny clothes and shoes as a thank you for their mysterious helpers (*everyone **measures** and **stitches** in the air, crafting imaginary tiny garments with care and affection*).

When the elves discovered the gifts, they were overjoyed and danced around the workshop in their new clothes (*everyone **dances** in a circle, **twirling** and **leaping** with happiness*). After that night, the elves didn't return, but the shoemaker and his wife never forgot the kindness and magic that had changed their lives. They continued to prosper and share their good fortune with others (*everyone **spreads their arms wide** to show sharing, then **shakes hands** or **hugs** a neighbour, symbolizing friendship, and gratitude*).

Warm-up: Have the children stand in a circle. Explain that they are going to warm up their bodies and imaginations by pretending to be different types of shoes. Call out the name of a type of shoe, such as a high heel, sneaker, or boot, and ask the children to move like that type of shoe. Encourage the children to use their bodies to copy the movements of the shoes as closely as possible, such as strutting like a high heel or jumping like a sneaker. After a few seconds, call out a new type of shoe and have the children switch to moving like that type of shoe. Keep calling out different types of shoes and encourage the children to be creative and playful with their movements. To make it more challenging, you can also ask the children to move in pairs or groups, and mime the movement of different combinations of shoes, such as a sneaker and a high heel together. To make it more interactive, you can also ask the children to take turns calling out types of shoes and leading the group in moving like that type of shoe.

Shoe suggestions:

High Heels: Strut confidently, taking high-stepped walks.

Sneakers: Jump around lightly, as if running or playing sports.

Boots: Stomp firmly on the ground, like walking through mud.

Ballet Flats: Glide gracefully, tiptoeing softly.

Rain Boots: Make loud, splashing steps as if walking through puddles.

Slip-on Sandals: Slide feet along the floor smoothly.

Tap Shoes: Create rhythmic tapping sounds with the feet.

Ice Skates: Glide and slide, pretending to balance on ice.

Flip Flops: Clap feet against the floor to copy the flip-flop sound.

Cowboy Boots: Walk with a swagger, like a cowboy with spurs.

Roller Skates: Roll and glide, swaying side to side.

Hiking Boots: Take exaggerated high steps, like climbing over rocks.

Snow Boots: Plod heavily, as if moving through deep snow.

Dance Shoes (Jazz): Do small jumps and kicks, showing off nimble footwork.

Soccer Cleats: Mime kicking a ball and running short distances.

Golf Shoes: Walk with short, precise steps, pausing to swing an imaginary golf club.

Platform Shoes: Pretend to be extra tall, walking carefully to maintain balance.

Barefoot (Beach): Tiptoe and stretch feet as if walking on hot sand.

Running Shoes: Run in place quickly, then slow down, simulating a sprint.

Gymnastics Slippers: Perform careful balance moves and simple spins.

Main Focus: *Talking Objects* - ask the children to choose an object from the story, such as a shoe, thread, or needle. Ask the children to imagine what the object might say or feel if it could talk. Encourage the children to use their creativity and imagination to come up with interesting ideas. Ask the children to take turns speaking for their object and improvising a short scene where it interacts with the other objects in the story.

Object Suggestions:

Leather: "I was just a plain piece of leather, but now I'm turning into something beautiful and useful!"

Shoe: "Once I was flat and lifeless, but now I can take someone on great adventures."

Thread: "Twisting and turning, I hold things together, making sure everything stays in place."

Needle: "I'm small but mighty, stitching the dreams of the shoemaker into reality."

Hammer: "With every tap and knock, I shape the destiny of shoes. It's a loud job, but someone's got to do it!"

Scissors: "I cut and shape, making the first moves in transforming leather into art."

Elf's Shoes: "We're the tiniest shoes with the biggest responsibility, helping our elf friends work their magic."

Workbench: "I bear the weight of creation, supporting the shoemaker and his tiny helpers in their craft."

Candle: "By my light, the late-night secrets of the workshop are revealed."

Glue: "I'm the silent hero, holding everything together, often overlooked but essential."

Ruler: "I measure twice so the shoemaker can cut once, ensuring every shoe is perfect."

Last (Shoe Mold): "Shoes take shape over me; I'm the foundation of every fit."

The Shoemaker's Glasses: "Through me, the world is brought into focus, helping to see the fine details of every shoe."

Paper Pattern: "I'm the first step in the journey from idea to shoe, a guide for the shoemaker's hands."

Cobbler's Apron: "I protect and serve, carrying tools and catching scraps, a silent partner in the dance of shoemaking."

Piece of Ribbon: "I add the finishing touch, a flourish of colour and style to delight the eye."

The Door to the Workshop: "I open to possibilities, welcoming those who enter with hopes and dreams of magical shoes."

Occupational Mime - ask the children to imagine they are the shoemaker. Ask the children to use occupational mime to show what the shoemaker might do during a typical day. Encourage the children to use their bodies to express different emotions, such as satisfaction, frustration, or exhaustion.

Occupational Mime suggestions:

Examining Leather: Stretch out hands, feel the texture and thickness of imaginary leather, turning it over and nodding approval.

Measuring and Marking: Hold an invisible ruler with one hand, and a pencil in the other, drawing lines across the leather.

Cutting Leather: Mime taking scissors, opening and closing them as you follow the lines you've drawn on the leather.

Punching Holes: Pick up an imaginary awl, press down into the leather to make holes for stitching.

Sewing Shoes Together: Thread an imaginary needle and pull it through the holes in the leather, sewing pieces together.

Applying Glue: Pretend to hold a brush, dipping it into glue and spreading it carefully along the edges of the shoe parts.

Fitting Soles to Shoes: Press the sole and the upper parts of the shoe together firmly, showing precision in alignment.

Polishing Shoes: Buff the shoes with a circular motion, using a cloth to bring out the shine.

Tidying the Workshop: Sweep the floor with a broom, then organize tools back onto an imaginary shelf.

Admiring Finished Work: Hold up a completed shoe, turning it around to inspect it from all angles, showing a look of satisfaction and pride.

Hot Seating - choose one child to play the role of the shoemaker. Ask the other children to take turns asking the shoemaker questions about his behaviour in the story, such as why he was struggling to make enough shoes, and how he felt when the elves helped him. Encourage the children to use their listening and communication skills to ask thoughtful questions and respond to the shoemaker's answers.

The following are examples of the questions that might be asked.

- How did you feel when you discovered that the elves had helped you make the shoes?
- Did you ever feel funny about accepting the help of the elves, given that you didn't know who they were or why they were helping you?
- How did you feel when you were poor?
- Looking back on the experience, how did it change your views on the value of hard work, kindness, and generosity?
- If you could say something to the elves now, what would it be?
- How did you feel when you realized that the elves had stopped coming to help you, and that you would need to rely on your own skills again?

- Did the experience of working with the elves change the way you treat others?
- What advice would you give to someone who is struggling in their work or have no money to buy food?

Teacher in Role - ask the other children to take turns acting out different scenes from the story, such as the shoemaker discovering the elves or the elves making the shoes at night. Encourage the teacher to play different characters in the story and interact with the children to help guide and shape the scenes.

Scene suggestions:

Discovering the Elves

Teacher's Role: The Shoemaker

Scene Description: After a long day of hard work, the shoemaker prepares the last piece of leather and goes to bed, hoping for a miracle. The next morning, he discovers a beautifully crafted pair of shoes on his workbench.

Example Interaction: As the shoemaker, show your surprise and wonder upon finding the shoes. Ask the children, "Who do you think made these wonderful shoes? How did they know exactly what I needed?"

The Elves Making the Shoes

Teacher's Role: Narrator or an Elf

Scene Description: Under the cover of night, the elves sneak into the workshop and begin crafting shoes with incredible speed and skill.

Example Interaction: If playing an elf, silently motion to the children to join you in the shoe-making process, mime sewing, cutting, and hammering. As the narrator, describe the elves' actions and ask the children, "How do you think the shoemaker will react when he sees the shoes?"

The Shoemaker's Gratitude

Teacher's Role: The Shoemaker's Wife or the Shoemaker

Scene Description: Overwhelmed with gratitude for the mysterious help, the shoemaker and his wife decide to stay up and catch the elves in action. They are moved to make clothes for the elves as a token of their gratitude.

Example Interaction: Discuss with the children, what gifts they would give to someone who helped them. Encourage them to mime creating tiny clothes and shoes for the elves, expressing thanks through their actions.

The Final Goodbye

Teacher's Role: Elf

Scene Description: After receiving the gifts from the shoemaker and his wife, the elves decide to leave, knowing their help is no longer needed. The shoemaker and his wife find the workshop empty but their hearts full.

Example Interaction: As an elf, explain to the children why it's time to move on and how the shoemaker and his wife have learned to stand on their own. Ask them, "What did the shoemaker learn from us? Why is it important to help others?"

Still Image and Flash Back/Flash Forward - ask the children to work in pairs or small groups.

Assign each group a scene from the story, such as the shoemaker's poor business or the elves helping him. Ask the children to create a still image that represents the key moment in the scene. Then, ask the children to create a flash back or flash forward to another moment in the story that relates to the scene they are depicting.

Here are some examples of scenes from the story of The Elves and the Shoemaker:

- The shoemaker and his wife struggling to make ends meet and deciding to use their last bit of leather to make a pair of shoes to sell.
- The shoemaker waking up the next morning to find the shoes already made and ready to sell, without knowing who made them.
- The shoemaker and his wife staying up all night to try and catch the elves in the act of making shoes.
- The shoemaker and his wife deciding to make clothes for the elves as a thank you for helping them.
- The shoemaker and his wife becoming successful and no longer needing the help of the elves.

Closure: *The Shoe Emporium* -Divide the children into small groups of 3-4 and ask them to come up with their own shoe designs based on the story of the Elves and the Shoemaker. Encourage them to be as creative and imaginative as possible. Once the children have designed their shoes, ask each group to present their designs to the rest of the class. Encourage them to explain how their designs were inspired by the story. After all the groups have presented, ask the children to work together as a class to create their own "shoe emporium". This can be done using props, costumes, and any materials you have available. Once, the shoe emporium is set up, have each child take turns pretending to be the Shoemaker and showcasing their shoe designs to the class. Encourage them to use their imagination and act out different scenarios. Finally, have a group discussion about the different themes and messages in the story, and ask the children to share what they learned from the workshop.

The Town Mouse and the Country Mouse Drama Workshop

Gather all the children in a circle. Once everyone is seated and comfortable, introduce the story of "The Town Mouse and the Country Mouse." The teacher explains that they will tell the story, and also describe movements that the children will act out together.

Movement Story:

Teacher: Once upon a time, a **Country Mouse** invited his cousin, a **Town Mouse**, to visit him in the countryside. The Country Mouse lived in a cozy nook under the roots of a big tree. He was proud of his home and eager to show his cousin the simple joys of country life. Let's start by making ourselves small, **curling up** like a mouse (*curl up small on the floor*). Now, let's **dig and scurry** around the floor to create our cozy home under the tree roots (*use hands to mime digging and make quick, scurrying movements around the space*).

But when the Town Mouse came to visit, he wasn't impressed. Instead, he invited the Country Mouse back to the town, promising to show him a world of luxury and abundance. Together, we **tiptoe and dash** across fields and meadows, pretending to dodge owls and foxes until we reach the bright lights and tall buildings of the town (*tiptoe quickly, then dash, miming sneaky and fast movements*).

In the town, the Town Mouse led the Country Mouse to a grand house where they found a feast left out in the dining room. There were cheeses, bread, fruits, and all kinds of delicious treats. Reach out and **grab** imaginary pieces of cheese, **slice** through bread, and **pick up** fruits. Bring the food close and pretend to **nibble** with quick, small bites, enjoying the rich offerings of the town (*mime grabbing, slicing, and nibbling movements*).

Suddenly, while enjoying their feast, a cat pounced into the room! The mice had to **dash and hide**, barely escaping with their lives (*jump back in shock, then sprint on the spot, diving into a safe spot and curling up small*). After the scare, the Country Mouse decided that the quiet, peaceful life in the country, with its simple food, was more to his liking. He didn't need the fancy foods of the town if it meant living in constant fear. **Stretch and yawn**, feeling the relief of returning to the open, peaceful countryside. **Stroll** slowly around, taking in the fresh air, and **settle down** into a comfortable, safe spot, feeling content and at peace (*stretch widely, yawn, stroll leisurely, then settle down comfortably*). Finally, celebrate the joy of simple country life with a **happy dance**, twirling and leaping freely, without a care in the world (*twirl and leap joyfully around the space*).

Warm-Up: In "Mousey Moves," children pretend to be mice, first exploring the calm countryside. They tiptoe, pretend to sniff and pick food, and curl up as if hiding when they hear "Cat!" This part lets them act like careful, curious country mice. Then, they switch to being town mice, moving fast, dodging, ducking, and jumping as if in a busy city. The "Cat!" shout makes everyone freeze or curl up, adding excitement. This warm-up gets children moving and ready for more activities, while they have fun imagining being mice in different places.

Main Focus: *Conscience Alley* – discuss the story, focus on the moment the Country Mouse decides whether to stay in the town or return to the country. Split the group into two lines facing each other, forming an alley. One child, playing the Country Mouse, walks down the alley while the others whisper advice or thoughts from the perspective of town or country life. This helps explore different viewpoints and the internal conflict of the Country Mouse.

Sculpting- in pairs, have children take turns sculpting their partner into statues that represent either the Town Mouse in a scene of luxury and abundance or the Country Mouse in a scene of simplicity and peace. Discuss the emotions and physical traits that might characterize the two mice and their environments.

Soundscape - divide the group into two smaller groups. One group creates a soundscape for the country, using their voices and bodies to make sounds you might hear in the countryside. The other group creates a soundscape for the town, with noises like car horns, bustling crowds, and other urban sounds. Discuss how the different environments affect the mood and feelings of the mice.

Thought Tracking - While children freeze in poses as either the Town Mouse or the Country Mouse during key moments of the story, tap them on the shoulder to invite them to share what their character might be thinking or feeling at that moment. This technique helps explore the characters' motivations and reactions to their situations.

Teacher: When the mice meet, we freeze and wonder, is the Country Mouse proud or shy about his home? Does the Town Mouse feel awkward or maybe a bit too proud? When they see the big feast in the town, we pause again. What's the Country Mouse thinking about all this food? Is he amazed or worried? And how does the Town Mouse feel showing all this off? Then, when the cat comes, we freeze one more time. What goes through the Country Mouse's head seeing such danger? And what about the Town Mouse? Does he think this is normal? Through these moments, we get to guess and share what the mice might be feeling, making the story richer and more fun.

Conclusion: *Circle Reflection* - Begin the closure by inviting each child to share their favourite moment or what they learned from the workshop. Pass around an imaginary "cheese" *(a simple ball or perhaps just a gesture)* as a talking piece to indicate whose turn it is to speak.

The Frog Prince Drama Workshop

Gather all the children in a circle. Once everyone is seated and comfortable, introduce the story of "The Frog Prince." The teacher explains that they will tell the story, and also describe movements that the children will act out together. Emphasize that their movements will help bring the story to life.

Words: Movement

- **Frog**: Crouch down and jump.
- **Prince**: Stand tall and place hands on hips, striking a regal pose.
- **Ball**: Mimic holding and bouncing a ball.
- **Splash**: Make a splashing motion with hands.
- **Kiss**: Blow a kiss.
- **Magic**: Wave hands in the air, mimicking a magical spell.
- **Castle**: Form a roof above your head with your hands.
- **Promise**: Cross your heart.
- **Leap**: Jump high with both feet.
- **Transform**: Spin around on the spot and then open arms wide.

Once upon a time, in a kingdom far away, a **prince** was turned into a **frog** by a wicked spell. He lived in a pond near a grand **castle**, longing for the chance to break the spell. One day, a young princess came to the pond, playing with her golden **ball**. Accidentally, she dropped it, and it fell into the pond with a **splash**.

The **frog** retrieved the **ball** and, in return, asked for a **promise** that he could live in the **castle**. The princess agreed, but once she had her **ball** back, she forgot her **promise** and ran back to the **castle**.

However, feeling guilty, she returned to the pond and honoured her **promise**. That night, at the **castle**, the **frog** shared her dinner and slept on a silk cushion. The next morning, when the princess awoke, she was surprised to see that the **frog** had transformed back into a **prince** with a **kiss**. It was a moment of **magic** as the **frog**'s curse was lifted.

Overwhelmed with joy, the **prince** and the princess **leap** and dance around the **castle**, their hearts full of happiness. The **transformation** was complete, and the **prince** was finally restored to his true form, ready to start a new life full of love and adventures.

Warm up: *Talking Objects-* Guide the children in a warm-up exercise where they pretend to be objects from the story, such as the golden ball, the well, or the palace. Encourage them to share their thoughts and feelings as these objects.

Talking objects suggestions:

Golden Ball - "I shine brightly in the sunlight and am the princess's favourite. But it's lonely at the bottom of the well, waiting for someone to find me."

Well - "I'm old and not many people think about me, but I hold deep secrets. When the golden ball dropped into me, I knew things were about to change."

Palace - "I have tall towers and big rooms where lots of stories happen. The frog prince's story was one of the most magical ones to come through my doors."

Crown - "I sit heavy on the king's head, seeing both good and bad choices. Having a frog wear me would be something completely new!"

Dining Table - "I'm where everyone gathers to eat and talk, usually holding royal meals. I never thought I'd have a frog sitting at me for dinner."

Silk Pillow - "I'm soft and comfy, giving everyone sweet dreams. But a frog dreaming of turning into a prince? Now, that's a heartwarming story."

Magic Spell - "You can't see me, but I can change things in big ways. Turning a frog into a prince really shows what I can do."

Rose Bush - "I grow the prettiest roses and see lots of secret talks and promises. My flowers are for love, even if my thorns sometimes get in the way."

Gate - "I separate the palace from everything else. I open up for many stories, but a frog turning into a prince. That's a special one."

Enchanted Forest - "I'm full of mystery with my whispering trees. The prince, who was once a frog, had quite the adventure through me."

Main Focus: *Role on the Wall* - draw the outline of a frog and a princess on large sheets of paper. Have the children suggest words and phrases that describe the characters and write them inside the outlines.

Improvisation: divide the children into small groups. Each group will create a short scene showing the princess meeting the frog and making a promise to be his friend in exchange for retrieving her golden ball.

Scene suggestions:

The Ball Drops - The princess is playing and drops her ball into the pond. The frog shows up and offers to get it back. This part is about their first surprise meeting and the frog's offer to help.

Making a Promise - Here, the frog asks to be the princess's friend if he gets the ball back. You can show the princess thinking it over and then saying yes, focusing on how important it is to help each other and keep promises.

Dinner Time - Pretend the frog comes to eat dinner at the castle, and everyone is surprised to see him. This can be a funny scene where everyone at the castle has to get used to having a frog at the table. It's all about being nice to new friends, even if they're different.

Turning Back into a Prince - This magical moment when the frog changes back into a prince can be full of excitement and happiness. It's a time to show how amazing things happen when you are kind and keep your promises.

Friends at Last- After the frog becomes a prince, you can show how he and the princess start being real friends. It's a good time to think about how being a good friend means liking someone for who they are, not what they look like.

Hot Seating - after the frog has transformed into a prince, the child playing the prince will sit in the "hot seat" and answer questions from the observers about their feelings, thoughts, and actions.

Improvisation - the children will create a short scene showing the prince and princess living happily ever after. Encourage them to explore how their characters have changed and grown as a result of their experiences.

Conclusion: *Magic Moments - i*nvite each child to share a magical moment they would wish for if they had the power of the frog prince's magic. It could be anything from flying like a bird to swimming like a fish!

Little Red Riding Hood Drama Workshop

Each child or group of children is assigned a specific word and action. The narrator reads the story aloud, and when the children hear their word, they must jump up and perform their action. The words are in **bold** to assist the teacher.

Word: Action

Skip: Pretend to skip along happily.

Pause: Freeze in place.

Run: Run in place as fast as you can.

Growl: Make a fierce growling noise.

Hug: Wrap your arms around yourself in a hug.

Hide: Crouch down low and cover your face.

Laugh: Giggle and clap your hands. **Surprise**: Gasp and hold your hands to your cheeks.

Once upon a time, there was a little girl named Little Red Riding Hood. One day, her mother asked her to take a basket of goodies to her grandmother, who lived in the woods. Little Red Riding Hood happily **skipped** along the forest path, humming to herself. Suddenly, she heard a strange noise and **paused**, looking around. It was the Big Bad Wolf, **hiding** behind a tree! He **growled** and leaped out, **startling** Little Red Riding Hood. She **screamed** and **ran** as fast as she could, the wolf chasing after her.

As she **ran**, Little Red Riding Hood remembered her mother's warnings to stay on the path and not talk to strangers. She **hugged** her basket tightly and tried to **hide**, but the wolf was too fast. Just when it seemed like all hope was lost, a woodsman appeared and scared the wolf away. Little Red Riding Hood **laughed** with relief.

Together, they continued on to grandmother's house, where they found her safe and sound. Little Red Riding Hood **hugged** her grandmother tightly, grateful for her safety. They **laughed** and shared the goodies from the basket, enjoying each other's company.

From that day on, Little Red Riding Hood was more careful in the woods, always remembering to stay on the path and listen to her mother's warnings. And whenever she heard a strange noise, she **paused** and looked around, ready for whatever **surprises** the forest might hold.

Warm-up: *mime-* Guide the children in miming different emotions (happy, sad, scared, and excited) and actions (walking, skipping, running, and tiptoeing) as if they are in the story.

Emotions

Worried: Wrinkle forehead, bite nails, pace back and forth.

Surprised: Open eyes wide, gasp, raise hands to cheeks.

Relieved: Exhale deeply, smile, pat chest.

Confused: Furrow brow, scratch head, look around in bewilderment.

Actions

Skipping: Lightly bounce on toes while moving forward.

Tiptoeing: Walk quietly on the balls of your feet.

Running: Pump arms back and forth while moving quickly.

Exploring: Look around with curiosity, touch objects, bend down to examine things.

Main Focus: Play a game of "Follow the Path" where children pretend to walk through the woods to Grandma's house, navigating imaginary obstacles like rivers, trees, and rocks... *Talking Objects:*

Assign each child an object from the story, such as Little Red Riding Hood's red cape, the basket of goodies, the forest path, or the wolf's disguise. Ask the children to imagine what their object might say or feel if it could talk. Red Riding Hood's Red Cape: "I'm warm and cozy, protecting Little Red Riding Hood from the cold forest."

Basket of Goodies: "I'm filled with delicious treats for Grandma, waiting to be delivered."

Forest Path: "I'm the winding trail through the woods, guiding travellers on their journey."

Grandma's House: "I'm a welcoming home, filled with love and warmth for all who enter."

Grandma's Quilt: "I'm a patchwork of memories, stitched together with love by Grandma's hands."

Grandma's Chair: "I'm the place where Grandma sits to knit, read, and watch the world go by."

Woodsman's Axe: "I'm a tool of the trade, used by the woodsman to keep the forest safe."

Wolf's Disguise: "I'm a cunning disguise, hiding the wolf's true intentions from unsuspecting victims."

Grandma's Spectacles: "I'm the glasses Grandma wears to see the world more clearly."

Flowers from the Forest: "We're the colourful blooms of the forest, brightening Grandma's home with our beauty."

Path Signs: "We're the markers along the forest path, guiding travellers safely to their destination."

Forest Animals (such as birds, rabbits, or squirrels): "We're the creatures of the forest, watching and listening to all that happens around us."

Grandma's Fireplace: "I'm the heart of Grandma's home, providing warmth and comfort on chilly nights."

Grandma's Knitting Needles: "We're the tools Grandma uses to create cozy blankets and warm socks for her loved ones."

Grandma's Tea Set: "We're the cups, saucers, and teapot that Grandma uses to enjoy a relaxing cup of tea."

Mime: Invite the children to imagine they are characters from the story, such as Little Red Riding Hood, her grandmother, the wolf, or even the trees in the forest. Ask them to use mime to show what their character might do during key moments in the story.

Scene suggestions:

Little Red Riding Hood setting out on her journey through the forest to visit her grandmother.

Little Red Riding Hood encountering the wolf for the first time in the forest.

The wolf tricking Little Red Riding Hood by asking her where she is going and learning about her destination.

Little Red Riding Hood picking flowers in the forest before continuing her journey.

The wolf running ahead to Grandma's house and pretending to be Little Red Riding Hood to gain entry.

Little Red Riding Hood arriving at her grandmother's house and noticing that something seems strange.

Little Red Riding Hood realizing the wolf has disguised himself as her grandmother.

Little Red Riding Hood's realization that the "grandmother" in bed is actually the wolf.

Little Red Riding Hood's escape from the wolf's clutches and her rescue by the woodsman.

Little Red Riding Hood and her grandmother's joyous reunion after the wolf is defeated.

Hot Seating: - choose one child to play the role of Little Red Riding Hood. Ask the other children to take turns asking Little Red Riding Hood questions about her actions and decisions in the story. Encourage the children to use their listening and communication skills to ask thoughtful questions and respond to Little Red Riding Hood's answers.

Examples of open-ended questions:

Why did you decide to go into the forest alone to visit your grandmother?

How did you feel when you first encountered the wolf in the forest?

Can you tell us what happened when the wolf approached you and asked where you were going?

What made you decide to stop and pick flowers in the forest? When you arrived at your grandmother's house, did anything seem strange to you?

What were your thoughts and feelings when you realized that the "grandmother" in bed was actually the wolf?

How did you manage to escape from the wolf's grasp?

What did you learn from your experience with the wolf in the forest?

If you could go back and change one thing about your journey, what would it be?

How do you feel now that you're safe and reunited with your grandmother?

Sculpting - the teacher will select a few children to "sculpt" other participants into positions representing the Wolf in Granny's bed, Little Red Riding Hood, and the Woodcutter. Other children will observe and give feedback. Once the positions are set, the sculpted children will perform a frozen tableau.

Closure: Gather the children in a circle and thank them for their participation in bringing the story of Little Red Riding Hood to life through drama. Then, lead them in a game called "Forest Freeze Dance." Play some lively music and encourage the children to dance around the circle like characters from the story, such as Little Red Riding Hood, the wolf, trees, and animals. When the music stops, call out a character or object from the story, and the children must freeze in a pose representing that character or object. Repeat this game a few times, allowing the children to express themselves creatively through movement and imagination. Finally, conclude the workshop by reflecting on the different drama activities they enjoyed and what they learned from exploring the story of Little Red Riding Hood in a fun and interactive way.

Suggestions:

- Little Red Riding Hood
- The Big Bad Wolf
- The Woodsman
- The Grandmother
- Trees
- Flowers
- Butterflies
- Birds
- Squirrels
- Rabbit
- Basket
- Red Cape
- Forest
- Path
- Picnic Blanket
- Wolf's Den

- Grandma's House
- Porridge
- Chair
- Bed

The North Wind and the Sun Drama Workshop

Once upon a time, the **North Wind** (*blow as hard as you can*) and the **Sun** (*shine brightly, spreading your arms wide*) were having a debate on who was stronger. They saw a **traveller** coming down the road, wrapped in a warm coat. They agreed that whoever could make the traveller remove his coat would be considered stronger.

The **North Wind** went first. He **blew** as hard as he could (*blow and wave your arms like the wind*), making a loud **growl** (*make a fierce growling noise*). The **traveller** felt the cold and **hugged** himself tightly, holding onto his coat (*wrap your arms around yourself in a hug*). But no matter how hard the North Wind blew, the traveller only wrapped his coat tighter to keep warm and decided to **skip** to keep his spirits up (*pretend to skip along happily*).

Seeing that the North Wind had failed, it was now the **Sun**'s turn. She **smiled** warmly and began to **shine** brightly (*smile and spread your arms wide to shine*). The air grew warmer and warmer, and the **traveller** started to **laugh** at the pleasant warmth (*giggle and clap your hands*). He felt so hot that he decided to **pause** under a tree (*freeze in place*) and **hug** himself in **surprise** at the sudden change (*gasp and hold your hands to your cheeks in a hug*).

As the Sun continued to **shine**, the **traveller** felt so warm that he decided to **run** in place to cool down (*run in place as fast as you can*). Finally, he **hid** his coat by taking it off and placing it beside him, choosing instead to **skip** along his way without the coat, enjoying the beautiful day (*crouch down low and cover your face, then pretend to skip along happily*).

The **North Wind** was **surprised** and had to admit that the **Sun** was stronger, not because of her force, but because of her gentle and warm approach (*gasp and hold your hands to your cheeks in surprise*). They both **laughed** and continued to watch over the Earth together, reminding everyone that kindness and warmth win over force and fear (*giggle and clap your hands*).

And so, the children learn that warmth and gentleness are powerful forces, just like how the Sun made the traveller remove his coat without using force, but by making him feel warm and comfortable.

Warm-up -begin with a physical warm-up activity to energize the children's bodies and spark their imagination. Lead them in simple stretches, followed by a game of "Mirror Mirror", where they pair up and mimic each other's movements. Afterward, play a game of "Emotion Charades" where each child takes turns acting out different emotions while the others guess.

Main Focus - *Talking Object* - divide the children into groups and assign each group an object from the fable, such as the North Wind, the Sun, the Traveler, or the Cloak. Ask the children to imagine what their object might say or feel if it could talk. Encourage them to be creative and come up with unique perspectives for their objects. For example:

North Wind: "I am strong and powerful, but sometimes my strength can be intimidating."

Sun: "I bring warmth and light to the world, making people feel safe and happy."

Traveler: "I am just a humble person trying to go about my journey, hoping for a peaceful day."

Cloak: "I am a shield against the elements, protecting the Traveler from the wind and sun."

Role on the Wall - draw the outline of the North Wind and the Sun on large sheets of paper. Have the children suggest words and phrases that describe each character and write them inside the outlines. This activity helps them understand the characters' motivations and traits. Some suggestions for words and phrases could include:

North Wind: Strong, Boastful, Forceful, Cold, Loud

Sun: Warm, Gentle, Radiant, Kind, Peaceful

Traveller: Vulnerable, Humble, Tired, Determined, Resourceful

Conscience Alley - create a "conscience alley" by lining up the children on either side of a clear path. Choose one child to play the role of the North Wind and another child to play the role of the Sun. Have them walk down the path while the other children offer encouragement and persuasion to the Traveler. Encourage the children to use persuasive language and emotional expressions to convince the Traveler to remove their cloak. Some examples of what the children could say:

North Wind: "Take off your cloak! My strength can easily blow it away!"

Sun: "Keep your cloak on. My warmth will make you comfortable without it."

Still Image -in small groups, ask the children to create a still image that represents a key moment in the fable, such as the North Wind boasting about its strength or the Sun shining warmly on the Traveler. Encourage them to use their bodies and facial expressions to convey the emotions and actions of the characters. For example:

North Wind: Children standing with arms outstretched, looking fierce and determined.

Sun: Children standing with arms open wide, smiling brightly with warmth.

Traveller: Child huddled with arms wrapped around themselves, looking weary but determined.

Hot Seating -choose one child to play the role of the Traveler. Ask the other children to take turns asking the Traveler questions about their experience with the North Wind and the Sun. Encourage the children to ask thoughtful questions and listen actively to the Traveler's responses. Some examples of questions they could ask:

How did you feel when the North Wind started blowing?

Why did you decide to take off your cloak?

How did you feel when the Sun started shining on you?

What did you learn from your encounter with the North Wind and the Sun?

Would you approach a similar situation differently in the future?

Conclusion: Gather the children in a circle and invite them to reflect on what they've learned from the fable. Discuss the moral of the story and how it relates to their own lives. Encourage them to think about times when they've experienced the power of kindness and gentleness versus forcefulness and aggression. End the workshop with a round of applause for their participation and creativity. You can also invite them to share any insights or personal connections they made during the workshop.

The Little Red Hen Drama Workshop

Assign specific words from "The Little Red Hen" story to actions. When these words are read out loud, the children will perform the corresponding action. This active participation helps reinforce key parts of the narrative and engages children in a kinaesthetic learning experience.

Word: **Action**

- **Plant**: Mime digging a hole and planting a seed.
- **Work**: Pretend to knead dough or perform other work actions.
- **Call**: Cup hands around mouth as if calling out.
- **No**: Shake head vigorously.
- **Grow**: Slowly stand up straight, starting from a crouching position, to mimic a plant growing.
- **Eat**: Pretend to hold food in your hand and bring it to your mouth.
- **Help**: Extend hands out as if offering assistance.
- **Sleep**: Rest head on hands and close eyes.
- **Wheat**: Make a waving motion with hands above head to represent wheat swaying in the wind.
- **Bread**: Rub belly and smile, indicating delicious food.

Once upon a time, **The Little Red Hen** found some grains of wheat and decided to **plant** them to make bread. She called to her friends, the Duck, the Pig, and the Cat, asking for help to **plant** the wheat. But each time, they would say **No** and **sleep** instead. So, the hen decided to **work** alone at each step, from planting the wheat, which began to **grow**, to harvesting it, and then to milling the wheat into flour.

When the wheat was ready to harvest, she again **called** to her friends, asking who would help her harvest the **wheat**. Again, they all said **No**. So, she **worked** alone to cut down the wheat and took it to the mill to be ground into flour. As she **worked**, she dreamed of the delicious **bread** she would make.

Finally, it was time to bake the **bread**. She **called** out for help once more, but her friends all said **No**. So, the Little Red Hen **worked** alone to bake the **bread**, which smelled so delicious as it **grew** golden and cooked through.

When the **bread** was done, she asked, "Who will help me **eat** the bread?" This time, her friends all said they would help. But the Little Red Hen said **No**, she would **eat** it with her chicks instead, for they had helped her by staying quiet while she **worked**.

And so, the Little Red Hen and her chicks **ate** the **bread**, enjoying the fruits of her labour, while her friends could only watch and wish they had offered to **help**. From that day on, they always offered to **help**, learning the value of hard **work** and cooperation.

Warm-up: Ask the children to stand in a circle. The teacher explains that she will start by doing a movement, and each child will copy it. After a few rounds of copying each other, start to challenge the children to come up with their own movements, such as crawling like a cat, jumping like a kangaroo, or spinning like a top. Encourage the children to use their imaginations and be creative with their movements.

Main Focus: *Role on the Wall* - draw a large outline of the Little Red Hen on a piece of paper or a whiteboard. Ask the children to suggest words or phrases that describe the Little Red Hen and write them on the outline. Next, draw a smaller outline of a character who is not helpful, such as the lazy dog or the greedy cat. Ask the children to suggest words or phrases that describe this character and write them on the outline. Discuss the differences between the two characters and how their actions affect the story.

Thought Tracking - choose a scene from the story where the Little Red Hen is working hard, and the other characters are not helping. Ask one child to play the role of the Little Red Hen and the others to be the other characters. Instruct the other children to freeze in a still image while the Little Red Hen expresses her thoughts out loud. Ask the other children to take turns being the Little Red Hen and expressing their thoughts while the others freeze in still images. Here are some examples of scenes from "The Little Red Hen":

- The Little Red Hen planting the wheat seeds in the ground.
- The Little Red Hen asking the other animals for help with harvesting the wheat.
- The Little Red Hen threshing the wheat to separate the grain from the straw.
- The Little Red Hen taking the wheat to the miller to make flour.
- The Little Red Hen asking the other animals for help with baking the bread.
- The Little Red Hen enjoying the freshly baked bread all by herself when the other animals refuse to help.

Sculpting – divide the class into groups of three. Assign each child a role: the Little Red Hen, the lazy dog, or the greedy cat. Instruct the children to sculpt their bodies to show their characters' physicality and how they relate to each other. Encourage the children to experiment with different poses and facial expressions to convey their characters' emotions.

Improvisation – divide the class into groups of 4. Assign each group a scene from the story. Instruct the children to improvise their own version of the scene, using the characters' dialogue and actions as a starting point. Encourage the children to be creative and come up with their own twists and turns in the story.

Flashbacks and Flashforwards - choose a scene from the story, such as when the Little Red Hen is planting and harvesting the wheat. Ask the children to create a still image of the scene. Then, ask the children to create a flashback to show how the wheat was planted, and flashforward to show how the wheat will be used to make bread. Encourage the children to think creatively and use their imaginations to come up with their own versions of the flashbacks and flashforwards.

Closure: *Group Performance* - divide the children into groups of five. Instruct each group to create their own performance of the Little Red Hen.

The Crow and The Pitcher Drama Workshop

Assign specific words from "The Little Red Hen" story to actions. When these words are read out loud, the children will perform the corresponding action. This active participation helps reinforce key parts of the narrative and engages children in a kinaesthetic learning experience.

Word: Action

- **Crow**: Flap arms at sides like wings.
- **Pitcher**: Make a wide circle with arms, creating the shape of a pitcher.
- **Water**: Wiggle fingers downwards to mimic falling water.
- **Peck**: Make a pecking motion with hand, as if being a bird pecking at seeds.
- **Thirsty**: Place hand on throat, looking exhausted or panting.
- **Stones**: Bend down to pick up an imaginary stone, then mime placing it into the pitcher.
- **Look**: Shade eyes with hand, pretending to look into the distance.
- **Fly**: Extend arms out wide and gently wave them up and down.
- **Drink**: Cup hands together and pretend to sip from them.
- **Think**: Tap temple with a finger, indicating a thinking gesture.

Movement Story:

Once upon a time, under the blazing sun, a **crow** (flap arms) searched desperately for water. "I'm so **thirsty**," the crow said, voice weak (place hand on throat). It soared over the land (extend arms and wave gently) until it spotted a **pitcher** (make a circle with arms).

Peering inside, the crow exclaimed, "Ah, **water** at last!" (wiggle fingers downwards) But its heart sank as it saw the water was too low. "Oh no, I can't reach it!" (shake head in dismay).

Suddenly, an idea sparked. "I know! I'll use **stones** to raise the water level," the crow **thought** aloud (tap temple). Off it flew (flap arms), returning with a small stone. "This should work," it muttered, dropping the **stone** into the **pitcher** (bend down and mime the action).

With each stone added, the crow chatted to itself, "Just a few more, and I'll be able to **drink**." It tirelessly worked (repeat the stone action), watching the water slowly rise.

After many trips, the crow cheerfully announced, "Yes, it's high enough now!" It leaned over the pitcher, finally able to **drink** the refreshing water (cup hands and pretend to sip). "Ah, that's much better. Where there's a will, there's a way!"

The crow, satisfied and no longer **thirsty**, concluded, "With a bit of thinking and a lot of effort, I can solve any problem!" Proudly, it flew off into the sky (extend arms and gently wave them up and down), ready for its next adventure.

Warm Up: *Rainstorm to Refreshment* - create a rainstorm through collective movement and sound, ending with finding imaginative ways to 'drink' the rainwater, connecting to the story's theme of seeking water. Have the children stand in a large circle, explaining that they'll be creating a rainstorm together. Begin the rainstorm with quiet movements, gradually building in intensity. Guide the children through the following steps, each for about 30 seconds to 1 minute:

Start with silence, then everyone rubs their hands together to mimic the sound of wind whispering. Progress to lightly snapping fingers, imitating raindrops starting to fall. Gently clap hands for the sound of steady rain. Softly stomp feet on the ground, representing the heavy downpour and thunder. Gradually reverse the order of the actions, moving from stomping back to silence, showing the storm calming down. Now that the rain has filled our imaginary pitcher, encourage the children to find creative ways to 'collect' and 'drink' the water. They can pretend to cup their hands to drink, use leaves to gather water, or even pretend to be animals lapping up the rainwater. Conclude with a quick circle time, asking how it felt to create the storm and find water, linking the activity to the crow's ingenuity in the story.

Main Focus: *Role-Play* - children are assigned roles, primarily the crow, but also potentially other animals that might offer the crow advice or observe its actions from afar. This encourages empathy and perspective-taking.

Suggested animals:

The Wise Owl - Perched high in a tree, the wise owl observes the crow's predicament. The owl might offer advice that encourages patience and observation. "Sometimes, the solution lies not in what we lack, but in how we use what we already have," the owl could say, suggesting a reflective and thoughtful approach.

The Eager Squirrel - Known for its quick movements and sharp eyes, the squirrel might suggest a more frantic search for water elsewhere. "Why not dash around and look for another source? There might be a stream or a pond nearby!" This reflects a more reactive, less considered approach, contrasting with the crow's methodical problem-solving.

The Lazy Tortoise - The tortoise, moving slowly towards a shaded area, might offer advice that speaks to perseverance and the slow but steady approach. "Take your time, little crow. Patience often brings its own rewards." This advice underscores the value of persistence over haste.

The Curious Rabbit - The rabbit, with its ears perked up, listening intently to the crow's dilemma, might suggest leveraging community resources. "Have you asked others for help? Sometimes, a problem shared is a problem halved." This introduces the concept of seeking assistance and the strength found in community.

The Ingenious Beaver - Known for its ability to alter its environment, the beaver might propose a more hands-on solution. "If I were you, I'd find a way to make that water come to me. Maybe there's a way to tilt the pitcher?" This advice leans into the theme of environmental manipulation and creative problem-solving.

Conscience Alley: -Form two lines of children facing each other, creating an alley. One child, playing the Crow, walks between the lines while the others, as the voice of the crow's thoughts, suggest different strategies to reach the water. This encourages exploring multiple solutions and the process of decision-making.

Still Image -In small groups, children create a tableau that captures a key moment in the story, such as the Crow's initial despair, the idea to use stones, or the success of raising the water level. This visual representation helps solidify the narrative's key points in the children's minds.

Key Moments that can be transformed into powerful still images or tableaus by children include:

The Crow's Discovery: The moment the crow first sees the pitcher, symbolizing hope or the potential solution to its thirst. Children could pose with expressions of curiosity and interest, one child mimicking the crow with outstretched wings leaning towards a child or object representing the pitcher.

Initial Despair: Capturing the crow's despair upon realizing the water level is too low to be reached. A child, representing the crow, could be posed looking into the 'pitcher' with a hand on the forehead in a gesture of frustration or disappointment, while others might observe from a distance to emphasize the crow's isolation.

The Idea: The pivotal moment when the crow gets the idea to use stones to raise the water level. This can be depicted by a child in the crow's role with a finger pointed upwards, a classic "eureka" gesture, while holding a stone in the other hand, with other children gathering around to watch the moment of inspiration.

Action: The crow beginning to drop stones into the pitcher. Children can create a dynamic scene with one child acting as the crow in the act of dropping a stone (another child could even be the stone, crouched and ready to be 'dropped'), highlighting the transition from idea to action. **Success:** The culmination of the crow's efforts when the water level is high enough to drink. This image might show the crow (child) 'drinking' from the pitcher with a look of relief or joy, while other children could represent the water, raising their hands to indicate the rising level. **Reflection:** After the crow has quenched its thirst, a moment of reflection on the perseverance and ingenuity it took to solve the problem. The child playing the crow could be seated, looking thoughtful or content, possibly surrounded by the other children representing the story's elements (stones, water, sun) in a circle of unity and accomplishment.

Conclusion: *Guided Visualisation* – Gather all the children and get to lie on the floor. Read the following: Close your eyes, and take a deep breath in... and let it out. Take another deep breath in... and let it out. Feel your body relax with each breath. Now, imagine you are standing in a warm, sunny field. You can feel the soft grass under your feet and the sun on your face. The sky above is a clear, bright blue.

In this field, you see a crow. The crow is feeling very thirsty on this hot day. It looks around for water and spots a shiny pitcher in the distance. Watch the crow as it flies over to the pitcher with hope. The crow peeks inside the pitcher and sees some water at the bottom, but it's too low to reach. The crow feels disappointed for a moment. Let's take a deep breath in with the crow... and let it out, releasing the disappointment.

Now, the crow doesn't give up. It pauses and thinks. As you breathe in, imagine a light bulb turning on above the crow's head. It has an idea! The crow decides to use small stones to raise the water level. See the crow as it picks up a stone and drops it into the pitcher. Splash! With each breath, imagine more stones being added. Splash... Splash... The water rises slowly. Notice how the crow feels hopeful with each stone it drops. It's working hard, but it's also staying calm and focused.

Finally, the water is high enough. The crow can drink! Feel the joy and satisfaction the crow experiences. Take a deep breath in to celebrate the crow's success... and let it out, feeling happy and refreshed. Let this story remind you that when you're faced with a challenge, you can find a solution by staying calm, thinking creatively, and never giving up. Just like the crow, you have the ability to solve problems and reach your goals.

Now, take one more deep breath in... and as you let it out, slowly start to bring your attention back to the room. Wiggle your fingers and toes. When you're ready, open your eyes. You're calm, refreshed, and ready to tackle any challenges that come your way.

Get the children to draw something they saw during the story. They bring their drawing back to the group and show it to their classmates.

www.ingramcontent.com/pod-product-compliance
Lightning Source LLC
Chambersburg PA
CBHW071639040426
42452CB00009B/1694